What Is the Story of the Headless Horseman?

by Sheila Keenan

illustrated by Andrew Thomson

Penguin Workshop

For the whole Keenan clan:
many heads, one heart—SK

For mum—AT

PENGUIN WORKSHOP
An imprint of Penguin Random House LLC, New York

First published in the United States of America by Penguin Workshop,
an imprint of Penguin Random House LLC, New York, 2023

Visit us online at penguinrandomhouse.com.

Library of Congress Cataloging-in-Publication Data is available.

Printed in the United States of America

ISBN 9780593523667 (paperback)   10 9 8 7 6 5 4 3 2   WOR
ISBN 9780593523674 (library binding)   10 9 8 7 6 5 4 3 2 1 WOR

Contents

What Is the Story of
the Headless Horseman? 1

The Father of American Literature 5

The Power of the Pen 24

The Mysterious Hudson Valley 34

Lost His Head 43

A Heart-Stopping Chase 61

Says Who? 79

American Accent 89

Thrills and Chills to This Day 99

Bibliography 106

What Is the Story of the Headless Horseman?

Every October, thousands of people flock to an area along the eastern shore of the Hudson River, about thirty miles north of New York City. They stroll down historic streets, imagining what life was like in the early days of the United

States. They *ooh* and *aah* at an amazing display of seven thousand carved and illuminated jack-o'-lanterns. Some huddle into horse-drawn wagons for haunted hayrides or hold candlelit lanterns high as they roam through the local cemetery.

The quaint small towns and villages in this region have a long history. They were established by Dutch and then English settlers on land first inhabited by the Weckquaesgeek people. Revolutionary War battles were fought there. But this is also a place where Halloween comes to life. It's the setting for America's first ghost story!

Welcome to Sleepy Hollow, New York, home of the Headless Horseman.

This dark, menacing figure on a rearing stallion charges through the pages of "The Legend of Sleepy Hollow," a famous short story by author Washington Irving. More than two hundred years after the story was first published, visitors still flock to Sleepy Hollow.

A classic edition of
The Legend of Sleepy Hollow and Other Stories

They're in search of the scary spots where key moments of the ghost story take place. Some of them no doubt secretly hope that the village's most famous resident will gallop by—and that they'll keep their heads if he does!

Washington Irving's story has thrilled generations of readers. But how did he come up with this terrifying tale and its terrible main character? And what in the world happened to that horseman's head?

The answers are part of America's own story!

CHAPTER 1
The Father of American Literature

Many historians call Washington Irving "The Father of American Literature." That's because at the time he wrote his popular books, articles, and short stories, the United States was a new country. Most literature taken seriously by educated people at that time was written and published by Europeans. A snobby English critic of the early 1800s asked, "In the four quarters of the globe, who reads an American book?"

Washington Irving

Everybody! Or at least it seemed like that after

Washington Irving started publishing his work. He became the first best-selling author in the United States and the first American to earn his living by his pen. He was a celebrity when the country itself was still celebrating having become an independent nation.

Irving was born in New York City on April 3, 1783. Just eight days later the Revolutionary War, which freed the American colonies from British rule, ended with a cease-fire. Washington Irving was named after the war hero who became the first president of the new nation. As a six-year-old, Irving watched the presidential inauguration of General George Washington in New York City, then the capital of the United States. He even met the famous man. Irving's nanny followed the president around lower Manhattan, with her young charge in tow. She finally cornered President Washington in a shop and introduced his namesake. George Washington patted Washington Irving on the head and blessed him.

The boy never forgot this, even when he became famous himself.

Washington Irving was the son of immigrants William Irving Sr., a sailor who had come from Scotland, and Sarah Saunders, from England.

William Irving Sr. became a successful merchant in New York City, importing and selling hardware, wine, and household goods. He and Sarah had eleven children. Washington was their youngest child.

As a boy, he lived with his family on William Street in lower Manhattan, a part of the city that was bustling and thickly settled. But young Washington liked to roam north along the Hudson River where the city turned into smaller

villages and open countryside. "I was always fond of visiting new scenes and observing strange characters and manners," he said. This curiosity came in handy when Washington turned to writing.

As a teenager, Washington Irving studied to become a lawyer. He needed a profession in order to support himself. But he was not a very dedicated student. Nor was he really interested in the law. Irving preferred going to the theater, accepting dinner invitations, traveling, and keeping up with an interesting circle of friends

and acquaintances. In 1802, when he was nineteen years old, he started writing letters that were published in his brother's newspaper. Readers enjoyed Irving's letters, which included theater reviews, funny descriptions of rowdy audiences, and mocking comments about marriage, fashion, and even dueling. He wrote these pieces using a pen name, a different name authors use to conceal their identity. Nonetheless, most people knew that printed letters signed by "Jonathan Oldstyle" were really written by Washington Irving. Pen names became a signature style for Irving in many of his later works.

Though he squeaked through the bar exam and became a lawyer, Washington Irving was still much more interested in dining, drinking, and gossiping about literature, culture, and politics.

These interests cost money, though. Irving wasn't all that excited about practicing law. And so he turned to writing.

In 1807, Washington Irving, his brother William, and some friends wrote and published  a literary magazine called *Salmagundi*. The articles in it poked fun at New York politics, well-known people, and the "fashionable world." *Salmagundi* was very popular; more and more readers became familiar with Washington Irving's writing. Two years later, he became an even bigger success.

Washington published his first major book, *A History of New York, from the Beginning of the World to the End of the Dutch Dynasty*, in 1809.

He was twenty-six years old. It is a very clever blend of history, geography, and satire (a writing style that uses humor and exaggeration to mock something). In *A History of New York*, facts can be funny and often aren't even factual! Irving's main intent was to poke fun at people who were too full of themselves,  expose social or political ideas that were false or insincere, and ridicule behavior that was too stuffy or snobby.

But he also was concerned with how Americans would establish the history of their new country, the United States. Washington Irving understood that "history" often reflects the point of view of whoever is explaining what happened.

Gotham

Batman fans know their hero lives in Gotham City, a fictional place. But Washington Irving was the first to use "Gotham" as a nickname for the real New York City.

In an essay in *Salmagundi*, Irving called his home city Gotham, which comes from an Old English word meaning "goat's town." Goats were

thought to be silly animals. So were the people who lived in Gotham, a real village in England. In the early thirteenth century, Gothamites pretended to be fools. At the time, foolishness was thought to be contagious or catching. People avoided the village. The Gothamites' trick kept the King of England—*and* his royal taxes—out of their village. Just as those clever Gothamite "fools" had intended all along!

In between the humorous sections of his book, Irving also asked what he called the "gigantic question": "What right had the first discoverers of America to land and take possession of a country, without first gaining the consent of its inhabitants . . . ?"

A History of New York is narrated by a character named Diedrich Knickerbocker, described as an eccentric "well-known Dutch historian." There was no such person in real life.

Diedrich Knickerbocker

Knickerbocker came straight out of Washington Irving's imagination.

The author also used the character of Diedrich Knickerbocker as a brilliant marketing tool to help sell his book. In October 1809, this notice and others like it appeared in several New York newspapers:

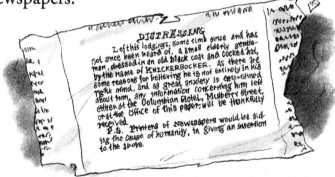

Left his lodgings, some time since, and has not since been heard of, a small elderly gentleman, dressed in an old black coat and cocked hat, by the name of Knickerbocker.

And readers paid attention! The missing man became a big topic of conversation and speculation in New York.

Knickerbocker Lives!

Because of Washington Irving's writing, people started using the word *Knickerbocker* for upper-class, snobby, or powerful New Yorkers, especially those with Dutch ancestors. Eventually, Knickerbocker became slang for New York City in general. It was used in naming everything from beer breweries to insurance companies to today's NBA basketball team, the New York Knicks. The fictional character, Diedrich Knickerbocker, became the city's unofficial mascot. He was usually shown wearing a colonial outfit, including a three-cornered hat. In 1936, "Father Knickerbocker" was even a giant balloon in the Macy's Thanksgiving Day Parade.

A few weeks later, in mid-November, another newspaper notice appeared. This one was from a man claiming to be Knickerbocker's landlord. The landlord said the old man had disappeared, owing rent. But he had left a "very curious kind of written book" in his room. If Knickerbocker didn't show up and pay up, the landlord was going to "dispose of his book to satisfy me for the same [overdue rent]."

Now New Yorkers were really intrigued: who—and *where*—was Diedrich Knickerbocker?

Nowhere to be found, it seems. So the "landlord" had the book published to pay off Knickerbocker's debt. Meanwhile, Washington Irving had invented the whole mystery, including the old man and his landlord, and had planted all the newspaper notices. His hoax paid off! Everyone was talking about Knickerbocker, and more importantly, they were buying copies of *A History of New York* hoping to learn more about him!

CHAPTER 2
The Power of the Pen

Although *A History of New York* was a success, Washington Irving did not yet think of himself as a full-time writer. In fact, he did not think of himself as a full-time anything in particular. He dabbled in the publishing world and in the political worlds of Albany, New York's state capital, and Washington, DC. He joined the New York State militia during the War of 1812 between the United States and Great Britain,

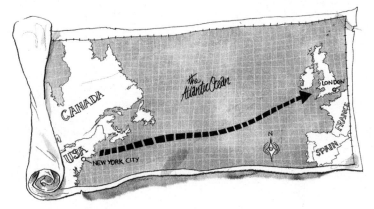

mostly writing dispatches for the general he served under. By 1815, he was in a slump. Washington convinced his brothers to finance a trip to Europe to renew his spirits and help him figure out what to do with his life.

From 1815 to 1832, Washington Irving lived in England and traveled throughout Europe. During those seventeen years abroad, he worked at his family's struggling merchant business.

He served on the staff of American foreign ministers in Spain and England. He befriended a number of authors and artists. And when he needed money, he wrote.

In 1819 the family business failed. Washington was still living in London. He thought about what he could publish to earn a steady income. He worked on an illustrated, revised edition of *A History of New York*, updating the original book that by then was ten years old. He also wrote essays and various stories, hoping to string them together and create another book. But the pieces weren't connected by any central theme. Irving thought of them as "sketches," a collection of stories rather than a longer novel.

Washington Irving started sending his writings in batches to his brother Ebenezer in New York City. He called the collection *The Sketch Book of Geoffrey Crayon, Gent.* Once again, Irving had created a fictional narrator for his work.

This time his pen name was "Geoffrey Crayon." He added the "Gent." for "gentleman."

The Sketch Book was originally published between 1819 and 1820 as a series of books. There were seven small paperback editions in America and two bigger hardcovers in England. The books were a hit with readers on both sides of the Atlantic! They were also financially successful, which was a relief to the author. Most importantly, the enthusiastic response to *The Sketch Book* proved that Washington Irving had finally made the right life decision: He was committed to earning his living solely by the power of his pen! Two of the editions of *The Sketch Book* include what are now Washington Irving's most famous tales, both set in New York State's Hudson Valley.

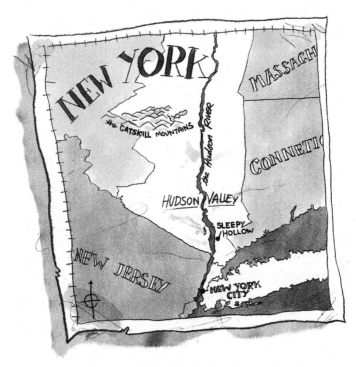

"Rip Van Winkle" appeared in the very first book. (Oddly enough, the publisher-printer's name was Cornelius S. Van Winkle!) The character in the title of this now widely known story is a Dutch American man who lives near the Catskill Mountains.

Rip Van Winkle heads to the hills to avoid his wife's nagging. Up in the Catskills, he meets some mysterious bearded men in old-fashioned clothes. They are drinking ale and playing a bowling game. The strange men offer Rip Van Winkle a swig from their keg. He falls asleep after drinking—and wakes up twenty years later!

Rip Van Winkle

Now with a beard a foot long, he wanders back to his village and finds he's missed the American Revolution, his wife has died, and his children are grown. The men he had met were actually ghosts!

Rip Van Winkle was a sleepyhead—but another character in a different story in *The Sketch Book* didn't even have a head! Washington Irving rode into wide and lasting fame with his character the Headless Horseman.

Merry Christmas

Halloween is when most people think of Washington Irving and his scary character with no head on his shoulders. But he had an important impact on another holiday, too: Christmas.

In *A History of New York*, Irving wrote a dream

Charles Dickens

sequence where Saint Nicholas, also known as Father Christmas, soared over treetops in a wagon full of presents for children. This idea turned into the classic idea of Santa Claus in his sleigh.

His short story collection with "The Legend of Sleepy Hollow" also includes Christmas stories. They take place in England but inspired what became American traditions. In the early 1800s, Christmas in the United States was not the elaborate holiday celebration it is today. Irving's stories described Christmas decorations and holiday parties where people sang carols and shared big feasts. This style of merrymaking caught on!

Irving may even have inspired the English author Charles Dickens to write his famous book *A Christmas Carol*. Dickens and Irving greatly admired each other's work and exchanged letters. The legendary authors met in person in New York City when Dickens first toured America in 1842.

CHAPTER 3
The Mysterious Hudson Valley

Washington Irving had loved the Hudson Valley since he was a teen. In 1798, he'd been sent to stay with friends in the area to escape a yellow fever epidemic in New York City.

The Hudson Valley was a beautiful region with deep woods full of birds and other animals, waterfalls cascading over rocky cliffs, the mysterious Catskill Mountains looming, and the wide, majestic Hudson River flowing. Washington Irving and his friends went hiking, swimming, and squirrel hunting. He also loved wandering through the valley's small villages where life seemed like that of an earlier era. Many settlers there had Dutch or German ancestors, and Washington heard ghost stories and tall tales from village elders. Some of those stories had roots in European legends. But over

time and many retellings, the details changed to reflect a New York State setting and a more American outlook. Washington Irving was an eager listener. As a young man, he "knew every spot where a murder or robbery had been committed or a ghost seen."

The dreamy, mysterious Hudson Valley landscape made a lasting impression on Washington Irving. Some of the places he visited in Europe as an adult reminded him of this exceptional area back home.

Irving was still living in England when the various editions of *The Sketch Book of Geoffrey Crayon, Gent.* were published. But it was the Hudson Valley he returned to when he wrote "The Legend of Sleepy Hollow," a story in the sixth volume of *The Sketch Book*. Irving set his story in the fictional town of Sleepy Hollow, a "little valley . . . a lap of land among hills" near a real place, Tarrytown. Sleepy Hollow was the perfect setting for his tale about a tall, skinny schoolteacher who's confronted by an even taller, scary Headless Horseman!

The Old Dutch Church of Sleepy Hollow

Early on in "The Legend of Sleepy Hollow," Washington Irving writes of the "drowsy, dreamy influence" of his story's setting. He compares it to "those little nooks of still water, which border a rapid stream . . . undisturbed by the rush of the passing current." Throughout the story, he mentions the landscape with its tall, old trees, chirping birds, cows in the pastures, ducks on the ponds, and the "amber clouds" over the "blue shadow of the distant mountain." Sleepy Hollow sounds like just that: a slow-paced, pleasant place to be.

Putting It on the Map

The actual village of Sleepy Hollow in New York State was once called North Tarrytown. According to Washington Irving's story, "Tarry Town," as it was originally spelled, was a nickname. Annoyed wives thought their husbands tarried (lingered) too long in the town tavern on market days.

In 1996, North Tarrytown renamed itself Sleepy Hollow to attract tourists. The town's logo is the Headless Horseman on his rearing stallion. The local football team is called the Horsemen and the Sleepy Hollow high-school newspaper is named *Hoofprints*.

Irving hints that something else might be afoot here. Lovely as the Hudson Valley village is, he also describes Sleepy Hollow as a place under "some witching power, that holds a spell over the minds of the good people." He claims its inhabitants are "given to all kinds of marvellous beliefs . . . and frequently see strange sights." And Irving is a master at transforming this sleepy town by day into a scary place by night!

The small birds that were fluttering and twittering in the light of day are replaced by loud screeching owls in the dark of night. The broad-branched autumn trees so beautiful in their "brilliant dyes of orange, purple, and scarlet" turn into gnarled, heavy overhanging boughs that groan as they scrape against one another in the wind. The woods seem haunted with "fearful shapes and shadows." In Sleepy Hollow, "there was a contagion in the very air that blew from that haunted region." Washington Irving carefully sets up the coming of nightfall in Sleepy Hollow.

The natural world that seemed so scenic now feels scary, especially if you are facing a long, dark journey home alone. It's no surprise at all that here you could easily run into a galloping ghost without a head . . . as the schoolteacher Ichabod Crane is about to find out!

CHAPTER 4
Lost His Head

It makes sense that storytelling would be a favorite pastime of the characters in a work called "The Legend of Sleepy Hollow." Whether at home or visiting neighbors, the fictional villagers in Sleepy Hollow love to gather by their firesides and entertain each other with bloodcurdling tales.

The stories they shared most often and most colorfully were about their own local bogeyman: the Headless Horseman of Sleepy Hollow.

This frightening figure galloped through the village on a large, powerful black stallion. The horseman himself was huge, too, and though he was "muffled in a cloak," one thing about him was inescapable: He had no head! The "most authentic historians of those parts" collected the "floating facts concerning this spectre [ghost]." They declared him to be the unearthly remains of a "Hessian trooper, whose head had been carried away by a cannon ball, in some nameless battle during the revolutionary war."

The Hessians were the thirty thousand German soldiers the British had hired to help them defeat the American colonists in the Revolutionary War. They were well-trained, fierce fighters. Hessians had a reputation for showing no mercy in battle and for looting as they marched through

Hessian soldiers

the countryside. Washington Irving's American readers at the time would have nodded *their* heads in agreement: Of course, the scary Headless Horseman would be a much-feared Hessian!

Heads Up!

Washington Irving may have been inspired by a real casualty at the Revolutionary War Battle of White Plains on October 28, 1776, or by one of the smaller skirmishes that followed on November 1. An American major general said he witnessed a shot from a cannon take off a Hessian's head.

Revolutionary War—era cannon

White Plains is not far from Sleepy Hollow. Irving makes a reference to the battle in "The Legend of Sleepy Hollow."

Not all Hessian soldiers thought of America as just a battleground. Some saw opportunity in this thriving country, which had a sizable German population. An estimated three to five thousand Hessians deserted and settled in the United States—presumably they all had heads!

As Washington Irving tells the story, the ghost soldier is supposedly buried in the cemetery in the Sleepy Hollow churchyard. Every night the Hessian rises from the grave, mounts his dark stallion, and thunders off in search of his missing head. Horse and rider are like a "midnight blast" past the village, through woods and swamps, over the hills, and onward to the battlefield. Searching, searching . . .

And still, no head.

The empty-handed Headless Horseman's return trip is even faster and more furious. He must race over a wooden bridge shaded by thick trees and make it back to the churchyard before daybreak.

Most villagers shuddered at the idea of running into this demon soldier, but they loved telling tales of his midnight rides. And Sleepy Hollow's new schoolmaster was an eager listener. "No tale was too gross or monstrous" for Ichabod Crane!

Ichabod Crane

Crane had recently arrived in Sleepy Hollow from Connecticut. Washington Irving has fun describing the new schoolmaster.

Crane is very tall and thin, with long arms and legs. He has "hands that dangled a mile out of his sleeves, feet that might have served for shovels." His nose sticks so far out from his face that his head looks like a weather vane. Ichabod Crane is a comical figure who looks like "some scarecrow eloped from a cornfield."

Nonetheless, he is a schoolteacher. In village society, Crane's education sets him above his farmer neighbors. Washington Irving pokes gentle fun at Crane's vanity. He says Ichabod clearly must be a man of learning because "he had read several books quite through." One of those books was about witchcraft, written by a New England minister named Cotton Mather.

Ichabod Crane was the master of the one-room schoolhouse. Outside of school, he moved from home to home in Sleepy Hollow. It was customary at the time for villagers to take turns hosting their schoolmaster, who did not get paid much. So every week, Crane lived and ate with the family of one of his students.

And skinny Ichabod liked to eat! Washington Irving describes him as feeding like a giant anaconda, one of the world's largest snakes!

Cotton Mather's Scary Stories

Cotton Mather was a famous minister, scientist, and one of the most influential thinkers of his time. Born in 1663 in Boston, Massachusetts, he enrolled in Harvard when he was twelve and graduated with a master's degree at eighteen. Over his long career, he wrote more than four hundred works on history, religion, medicine, and the sciences. He was the kind of person who believed in the lifesaving potential of smallpox vaccinations but also in the evil power of witches and devils.

Mather also wrote about the Salem witch trials of 1692–1693 and the people in that Massachusetts town who were accused, jailed, tortured, and executed for practicing witchcraft. In Irving's story, Ichabod Crane "most firmly and potently [strongly] believed" everything Cotton Mather wrote on the subject.

In return for all the food and the lodging, Crane helped out with farm chores and with entertaining the children in the family. He liked making the rounds in Sleepy Hollow. And village women liked him! "The schoolmaster is generally a man of some importance in the female circle of a rural neighbourhood." Ichabod Crane arrived like "a kind of travelling gazette [newspaper], carrying the whole budget of local gossip from house to house."

Crane liked trading what news he had for the delicious tea and treats the local women provided. But much as he loved talking and eating, he also loved listening to scary stories being told. Ichabod Crane spent many evenings at houses around town "snugly cuddling in the chimney corner of a chamber that was all of a ruddy glow from the crackling wood fire." There he and his neighbors roasted apples and swapped scary stories about "ghosts and goblins, and haunted fields and haunted brooks, and haunted bridges and haunted houses." The most terrifying stories of all, of course, were sightings of the headless one, the "galloping Hessian of the Hollow, as they sometimes called him."

When it was his turn to tell chilling tales,  Ichabod Crane was ready! He spoke of omens such as comets and shooting stars. He knew all about witches and the devil's work from his prized possession, the book by Cotton Mather. After listening to the villagers spin their tales, Crane "repaid them in kind with large extracts from his invaluable author."

The schoolmaster thoroughly enjoyed these evenings—right up until the moment when it was time to leave. Ichabod Crane then had to walk alone in the dark to whichever household he was boarding with. "What fearful shapes and shadows beset his path . . . how often was he thrown into complete dismay by some rushing blast, howling among the trees?" Needless to say: Ichabod Crane walked *very quickly*!

He sang hymns all the way home, to boost his courage and keep away evil spirits!

But then by morning's light, the schoolmaster forgot his terror. In time, he even forgot about the Headless Horseman. Ichabod Crane was bewitched by someone else: He was in love!

CHAPTER 5
A Heart-Stopping Chase

Katrina Van Tassel, a local young woman with rosy cheeks, had captured Ichabod Crane's "soft and foolish heart." The schoolmaster now thought less about a soldier ghost raging through the night. Instead, he focused on wooing Katrina, especially after he visited her at home. Ichabod was in love with the young woman *and* her mansion, wealth, and the big prosperous farm she would inherit from her doting father.

Katrina Van Tassel

Ichabod Crane visits the Van Tassel farm, which he coolly assesses in terms of food.

The snowy geese floating on a pond he pictures as cooked and "swimming in their own gravy." The "sleek unwieldy porkers" in the pigpen fill him with thoughts of bacon, juicy hams, and a roasted stuffed pig with an apple in its mouth. The fruit-filled orchards, fertile fields, and

spacious Van Tassel home make "the conquest of
his heart" complete. Crane easily sees himself as
Katrina's husband, living in luxury. There's just
one problem: How will he win her affections?

Ichabod has serious competition for the hand
of Katrina Van Tassel. She is a charming girl, and

there are many young men vying for her attention. One of them literally stands above the rest.

Abraham Van Brunt is a large, strong, fun-loving, mischievous villager. "From his Herculean frame and great powers of limb, he had received the nickname of Brom Bones."

Abraham Van Brunt

Brom is a daring and skilled horseman. His Sleepy Hollow neighbors "looked upon him with a mixture of awe, admiration, and good will." And if there was a brawl or a prank or any whooping and hollering going on, they knew who would be leading the charge: Brom Bones.

Ichabod Crane took advantage of the fact that he was the singing teacher for the village. He visited Katrina often for voice lessons, which also meant he could take her on walks and try to impress her with his affections. Brom Bones fumed. Before Ichabod came along, he had the best chance with Katrina. Bones began annoying the schoolteacher and playing tricks on him. He even taught his dog to whine in imitation of Ichabod's singing!

Both men were invited to a big party at the Van Tassel home. Ichabod Crane stuffed himself with the meats, chicken, fish, pies, and cakes. "He could not help, too, rolling his large eyes round him as he ate, and chuckling with the possibility that he might one day be lord of all

this scene." Then he began "clattering about the room," dancing with Katrina. Meanwhile, Brom Bones sulked in a corner.

Eventually, Ichabod Crane joined a group that was swapping Revolutionary War stories. As the evening wore on, they turned to ghost stories.

Ichabod, for Real!

Ichabod is a name that comes from the Bible. Even in Washington Irving's time, it wasn't very popular or commonly used. But there was a real, live Ichabod Crane.

Colonel Ichabod B. Crane (1787–1857) was born in New Jersey and is buried in Staten Island, a borough of New York City. He was a respected military man for forty-eight years. During the War

of 1812 both Crane and Irving served under the same commander at a fort on Lake Ontario. It's not known for sure if the two men ever met in person, but the name certainly has lived on!

Ichabod B. Crane

In one scary tale, the Headless Horseman forced an old man up onto his blazing stallion. Together they galloped through the countryside. When they reached the bridge near the church cemetery, the Horseman suddenly turned into a skeleton and tossed the old man into the brook. The bony rider and his ghost horse then "sprang away over the tree tops with a clap of thunder."

Not to be outdone, Brom Bones jumped in.
He boasted of *his* adventure with the Headless
Horseman. He said the Hessian spirit had
overtaken him one night as Bones rode home
on his steed, Daredevil. The young man boldly
challenged the dead man to a horse race. Bones
claimed he would have won, too. But just as they
got to that bridge near the church, the Headless
Horseman "vanished in a flash of fire."

The hour was late, the Van Tassel party broke up, and all the tales told "sunk deep in the mind of Ichabod." Still, the schoolmaster didn't leave the mansion, even when the "late scene of noise and frolick was all silent and deserted." He went to talk to Katrina, convinced that he would be successful in his marriage proposal to her.

Things did not work out. Why? The author does not explain. So heavyhearted Ichabod left for home, riding on a borrowed broken-down old horse, alone at the "very witching time of night."

The stirrups were too short, so his knees were scrunched up high. His "sharp elbows stuck out like grasshoppers'." His long black coat "fluttered out almost to the horse's tail." Ichabod Crane was a comical sight. What he was about to see was not!

Ichabod approached a stream said to be haunted. The old horse he rode stopped and refused to budge. He heard a splash in the dark. He peered into the shadows at the edge of the brook . . . and then he saw it: something "huge, misshapen, black and towering . . . like some gigantic monster ready to spring."

Crane's hair stood on end. He stammered, "Who are you?" There was no reply. (Spoiler alert: It's hard to answer a question when you don't have a mouth!) What Ichabod saw appeared to be "a horseman of large dimensions, and mounted on a black horse of powerful frame." The schoolmaster took off.

Ichabod Crane tried to lose the mysterious
horseman, who stayed parallel with him on the
other side of the brook. Crane rode faster, then
slower, then fast again. The dark, silent horseman
adjusted his speed each time to keep pace. Then
the two rode up a hill. The unknown horseman

was silhouetted against the sky. "Ichabod was horror struck." His unwanted riding companion had no head on his shoulders! Even worse, the horseman *was carrying* his head at the front of his saddle!

Ichabod Crane urged his horse forward as fast as the creature would go. The Headless Horseman dashed right after him. The race was on. Crane lost his saddle and was slip-sliding off his horse.

He wrapped his arms around the horse's neck and held on for dear life.

The Headless Horseman kept coming.

Ichabod saw the church bridge up ahead. He remembered what Brom Bones said about the demon disappearing there. "'If I can but reach that bridge,' thought Ichabod, 'I am safe.'"

He felt the hot breath of the ghost horse behind him.

Ichabod Crane thundered across the bridge. Just as he reached the other side, he turned to see if the ghoul had vanished as he should, in a "flash of fire and brimstone."

He had not.

The enormous Headless Horseman rose high in his stirrups and hurled *his head* at the schoolmaster! "Ichabod endeavoured [tried] to dodge the horrible missile, but too late."

CHAPTER 6
Says Who?

The next morning, no schoolmaster came down for breakfast with his host family. No teacher waited for the children at the schoolhouse. There was no sign of Ichabod Crane at all.

There was only a tired old horse that returned to its stable without its saddle. The horse's owner and some villagers organized a search and found the saddle in the road leading to the church, trampled. They spotted deep hoofprints leading to the bridge. And then, beyond the bridge, on the bank of the brook, they discovered Ichabod's hat—*next to a shattered pumpkin*!

What they didn't find was the schoolmaster himself.

Ichabod Crane was never seen in Sleepy Hollow again. His few belongings, including some feeble attempts to write love poems to Katrina Van Tassel and his precious Cotton Mather book, were thrown away and burned. After Sunday church services, the villagers went to the spot where the hat and the pumpkin were found. They considered the strange disappearance. They weighed all the different explanations. They shook their heads and came to the only possible conclusion: Ichabod Crane had been carried off by the Headless Horseman. Then "nobody troubled his head any more about him" and the villagers hired a new schoolteacher.

"The Legend of Sleepy Hollow" ends in mystery. Whenever Ichabod Crane and the smashed pumpkin were mentioned, Brom Bones

(who eventually did marry Katrina) laughed heartily and looked "exceedingly knowing . . . which led some to suspect that he knew more about the matter than he chose to tell." Brom had always liked to tease and embarrass the schoolteacher. Maybe *he* had chased Crane in the dark and tossed the pumpkin.

Occasionally, rumors were heard about Ichabod. That he was alive, but too embarrassed to remain in Sleepy Hollow when Katrina rejected his marriage proposal. Or that he had been so terrified of the Headless Horseman that he left town. Or that he had moved far away and become a lawyer or a journalist.

Ichabod Crane, who had so loved all the eerie storytelling around the fire, became a character in one of those very stories. Some villagers claimed to hear Crane's ghost singing sadly near the schoolhouse. But it was the tale of the Headless Horseman spiriting away the unlucky schoolteacher that became "a favourite story often told" in Sleepy Hollow.

Washington Irving suggested several possible ideas as to what happened that dark night when Ichabod Crane encountered the terrifying Hessian without a head. He also used several narrators to tell "The Legend of Sleepy Hollow."

It's All in the Details

One man captured the Headless Horseman—in a painting, that is! American artist John Quidor (1801–1881) was inspired by Washington Irving's stories. His oil painting "The Headless Horseman Pursuing Ichabod Crane" (1858) now hangs at the Smithsonian American Art Museum in Washington, DC. In it, Quidor shows what he thinks happened at the end of "The Legend of Sleepy Hollow": His Headless Horseman is clearly throwing a pumpkin!

Irving is, of course, the real author of *The Sketch Book of Geoffrey Crayon, Gent.*, the collection that includes "The Legend of Sleepy Hollow." Even though it sounds like *The Sketch Book* was written by Geoffrey Crayon, he is yet another character Washington Irving made up. Irving tries to be very convincing about this: the first piece in *The Sketch Book* is "The Author's Account of Himself"—by Geoffrey Crayon!

At the beginning of "The Legend of Sleepy Hollow," there is a note under the title declaring this story was "Found Among the Papers of the Late Diedrich Knickerbocker."

Knickerbocker, once again! At the end of "The Legend of Sleepy Hollow," there is a final note, called a postscript. It is signed by "D.K." In the postscript Knickerbocker claims he heard the whole Headless Horseman story from a "shabby, gentlemanly old fellow" at a business meeting in Manhattan. When this old man is quizzed about the truth of the fantastic tale he just told, he replies, "I don't believe one half of it myself."

"The Legend of Sleepy Hollow" is constructed as a story within a story within a story. Just like there are several possible endings to the tale, there are several possible ways it came to be told. Geoffrey Crayon found the story written up in the papers of Diedrich Knickerbocker, who wrote down what he heard from an old man from the countryside who doesn't even fully believe the story he just told! And none of these characters are real; they were all created by the actual author. By using this technique, Washington Irving masterfully shows how legends survive and thrive. They are told and retold, passed along from person to person, changing with each telling, until no one can claim to know what "really" happened. By using this writing style, Washington Irving can be playful with the "truth" of his story, should anyone question it. He can also provide funny comments about people, places, and the plot as it unfolds. Not to mention the humor of having several narrators in a story whose villain, the Headless Horseman, never speaks!

CHAPTER 7
American Accent

"The Legend of Sleepy Hollow" was first published on March 15, 1820, in the sixth volume of *The Sketch Book of Geoffrey Crayon, Gent.* The United States was not even fifty years old. Some people who had experienced the Revolutionary War were still alive!

Revolutionary War veteran

US flag, 1820–1822

This new country had once been several European colonies. So it made sense that American culture had always been influenced by European styles and customs. For example, you could find traces of German and Dutch folktales in "Rip Van Winkle" and "The Legend of Sleepy Hollow." But the people of the United States were eager for art and literature that reflected an American point of view. And Washington Irving delivered!

Irving was a very funny storyteller, whose use of history and geography created a new American storytelling sensibility. In a letter to a friend, he wrote, "I am endeavoring [trying] to serve my country—Whatever I have written has been written with the feelings and published as the writing of an American. If I can do good in this world it is with my pen." And Washington Irving *did* do good! His writing contributed to British and other European readers acknowledging that American literature was worth reading. One British historian wrote of *The Sketch Book*: "Everywhere I find in it the marks of a mind of the utmost elegance and refinement, a thing as you know that I was not exactly prepared to look for in an American."

Irving offered his fellow citizens literature with an American point of view. He included geographical details that firmly established his stories like "Rip Van Winkle" and "The Legend of Sleepy Hollow" took place in the United States. He provided so many background details that were inspired by American history. For example, Irving described the residents of Sleepy Hollow as "descendants from the original Dutch settlers." The Headless Horseman is an imaginary enemy soldier. But he rides off nightly in search of his head in an area where real battles of the American Revolution had been fought. Meanwhile, Ichabod Crane has American roots, too. He originally comes from Connecticut. And one of the scarier places mentioned in "The Legend of Sleepy Hollow" is a "great tree" that "towered like a giant above all the other trees of the neighbourhood." During the Revolutionary War, British major John André was hanged from the huge, gnarled limbs of this tree after he was found guilty of plotting with American general Benedict Arnold. They planned to betray the American forces stationed at a fort at West Point, New York.

You Get What You Pay For

Some readers complained that *The Sketch Book of Geoffrey Crayon, Gent.* cost too much. In a letter to a friend, Washington Irving argued back: "If the American public wish to have literature of their own, they must consent to pay for the support of authors."

He understood that publishing was a business. And if American literature was going to thrive, American authors had to survive! He was influential in helping preserve copyrights, the legal licenses authors hold to protect earnings on their works.

Irving acknowledged the power money held in American culture. In a short story published in 1837, he coined the now familiar phrase "the almighty dollar."

The almighty dollar, that object of universal devotion
-WAshington Irving

Major John André

Ever since André's execution, villagers claimed to have heard moaning and been startled by "strange sights" near this tree in Sleepy Hollow.

Washington Irving's descriptions of food and shelter in "The Legend of Sleepy Hollow" also help build a picture of life in the United States. Irving describes Katrina Van Tassel's home as "one of those spacious farm houses, with high ridged, but lowly sloping roofs, built in the style handed down from the first Dutch settlers."

This is the kind of architecture you would have seen in the Hudson Valley at the time. (And you can still see some buildings from that time, including Washington Irving's home, called Sunnyside, in Tarrytown, New York.)

Sunnyside

American readers would easily recognize the mention of local food. Villagers in Sleepy Hollow eat hasty pudding. This traditional dessert was made of boiled ground cornmeal and often molasses. They also like their cornmeal slapjacks, a kind of pancake. Ichabod Crane fantasizes about both of these foods when he rides past cornfields. And he's delighted to see plenty of "oly koek" is on the table at the Van Tassel party. Irving is credited with possibly making this Dutch treat popular in the United States. It still is: *Oly koek* is a donut! Even the mystery of what the Headless Horseman threw at the end of the story— his head or a pumpkin— has a national connection.

Oly koek

Pumpkin is a fruit that originated in the Americas.

American readers appreciated seeing their new country reflected in Washington Irving's books. Readers in both the United States and Europe made the original multivolume publication of *The Sketch Book of Geoffrey Crayon, Gent.* a success.

Irving earned a considerable amount of money from both the American and British editions. He revised and republished *The Sketch Book* in 1848. Again it was a best seller. Washington Irving was so popular that people bought prints of his portrait to frame.

Readers and critics praised Irving's stories and essays. They especially enjoyed the shivery thrill of "The Legend of Sleepy Hollow." Irving called this story "a random thing." But nineteenth-century readers loved its atmospheric mood, its comical, bumbling schoolteacher, and its bloodcurdling phantom—and readers still do today.

CHAPTER 8
Thrills and Chills to This Day

The Headless Horseman rode out of the pages of Irving's nineteenth-century story into modern culture and media.

Moviemakers were inspired by the story of the heart-stopping Hessian without a head who scared a schoolteacher out of his wits. In the 1920s, three silent films adapted the story. A 1949 Disney film called *The Adventures of Ichabod and Mr. Toad* is based on two classic works, "The Legend of Sleepy Hollow" and *The Wind in the Willows*. In this full-color animation, a famous singer, Bing Crosby, narrated the legend and was the voice of Ichabod Crane. The popular film was later shown on television; it was more funny than scary.

Modern filmmaker Tim Burton, on the other hand, went for all-out horror in 1999's *Sleepy Hollow*, starring Johnny Depp as Ichabod Crane. In Burton's film, the landscape is enveloped in a constant eerie fog, skulls appear in the flames of a fireplace, and the Headless Horseman charges out of a massive, gnarly old "Tree of the Dead." He gallops through the woods on his midnight-black stallion with a gleaming sword held high, chases down unlucky villagers, then lops off their heads. Burton added a gruesome detail to these scenes: The heads spin as they hit the ground!

The Headless Horseman also appears as a villain in several animated *Shrek* movies from DreamWorks. At the end of *Shrek the Third* (2007), Washington Irving's scary character tearfully reveals a heartfelt wish: "I've always wanted to play the flute." It's a very funny line for someone without a head!

"The Legend of Sleepy Hollow" was also a creative source for the television series *Sleepy Hollow*, which aired from 2013 through 2017 on the Fox network. This series used Washington Irving's story and characters as a starting point.

It even had a touch of Rip Van Winkle. In the *Sleepy Hollow* television show, Ichabod Crane wakes up in Sleepy Hollow, New York, in 2013— and so does his enemy, the Headless Horseman.

Final Rest

Washington Irving wrote that if you wanted to escape "the world and its distraction," there was no place better than Sleepy Hollow. Clearly this was a fitting place for eternal rest!

Irving died at his beloved home near Tarrytown on November 28, 1859. On December 1, bells in New York City tolled and flags were lowered to half-mast. The city courts closed so people could take the train to the funeral. More than a thousand mourners paid respects at the casket. A procession of 150 carriages followed the coffin to the Sleepy Hollow Cemetery, right by the Old Dutch Church. Irving was buried in the very place he made famous!

The iconic rider without a head and his hell-bent horse have been reproduced on everything from Halloween decorations to US postage stamps to weather vanes. Gamer fans of *Minecraft*, *Assassin's Creed*, *Call of Duty*, and *World of Warcraft* can see the Headless Horseman tossing a flaming pumpkin head or wielding a deadly sword or broadax in editions of these video games.

And, of course, the legend remains in print in books for children and adults.

People still love the thrills and chills of the scary story of the dark, silent soldier on his thundering stallion. Because there's always the chance that on a visit to Sleepy Hollow you might pass by the eighteen-foot-high steel sculpture of the Headless Horseman tossing a grinning jack-o'-lantern at poor Ichabod Crane—and then feel the "midnight blast" of the wicked ghost rider coming your way!

Bibliography

*Books for young readers

*Algar, James, Clyde Geronomi, and Jack Kinney. ***The Adventures of Ichabod Crane and Mr. Toad*** (includes "The Legend of Sleepy Hollow"). 1949. Burbank, CA: Walt Disney Animation, 2014. DVD.

Burton, Tim, dir. ***Sleepy Hollow***. 1999. Hollywood, CA: Warner Brothers, 2000. DVD.

*DK Eyewitness. ***American Revolution***. New York: DK Children, 2022.

Irving, Washington. ***The Legend of Sleepy Hollow and Other Stories [The Sketch Book of Geoffrey Crayon, Gent.]***. New York: Penguin Books, 2014.

*Irving, Washington. ***The Legend of Sleepy Hollow and Rip Van Winkle***. Mineola, NY: Dover Publications, 1995.

*Irving, Washington. *Rip Van Winkle and The Legend of Sleepy Hollow: Illustrated 200th Anniversary Edition*. Orinda, CA: SeaWolf Press, 2020.

Jones, Brian Jay. *Washington Irving, An American Original*. New York: Arcade Publishing, 2008.

Various directors. *Sleepy Hollow: The Complete Seasons 1–4*. 2013–2017. Los Angeles, CA: Twentieth Century Fox Television, 2017. DVD.

Websites

www.hudsonvalley.org/historic-sites/washington-irvings-sunnyside/

www.visitsleepyhollow.com

Timeline of the Headless Horseman

WHO HQ

Timeline dates: 1775–83 · 1783 · 1798 · 1802 · 1807–08 · 1809 · 1812–15 · 1814 · 1815–32 · 1819 · 1819–20 · 1820 · 1842 · 1848 · 1858 · 1859 · 1949 · 1999 · 2004–07 · 2013–17

Washington Irving born in New York City on April 3

Irving's first writing published: letters to his brother's newspaper

The War of 1812 between the United States and Great Britain

Lives in England and travels through Europe

The Sketch Book of Geoffrey Crayon, Gent. published in several volumes; Volume 1, published on June 23, 1819, includes "Rip Van Winkle"

The Sketch Book of Geoffrey Crayon, Gent. revised edition published

Washington Irving dies on November 28

Sleepy Hollow movie, directed by Tim Burton, released

Salmagundi magazine published

Irving serves in the New York State militia

Irving's funeral is held on December 1

Headless Horseman appears as a character in *Shrek* animated movies

Stays in the Hudson Valley to escape yellow fever epidemic

Washington Irving and Charles Dickens meet in New York City

Disney's *The Adventures of Ichabod and Mr. Toad* movie released

The Irving family's merchant business fails

Sleepy Hollow television series airs on the Fox network

The American Revolutionary War

A History of New York, from the Beginning of the World to the End of the Dutch Dynasty first published; revised editions published in 1812, 1819, and 1848

The Sketch Book, Volume 6 published on March 15; includes "The Legend of Sleepy Hollow"

John Quidor paints "The Headless Horseman Pursuing Ichabod Crane"

HISTORY OF NEW-YORK, FROM THE BEGINNING OF THE WORLD TO THE END OF THE DUTCH DYNASTY. By Diedrich Knickerbocker. THE AUTHOR'S REVISED EDITION. New York: G. P. PUTNAM & CO., 321 BROADWAY. 1857.

THE SKETCH BOOK OF GEOFFREY CRAYON, GENT. WASHINGTON IRVING

Photo credits (from left to right): powerofforever/DigitalVision Vectors/Getty Images; traveler1116/DigitalVision Vectors/Getty Images; public domain, via Library of Congress (LCCN 25014699); public domain, via Library of Congress (LCCN 00004730); Chris Hellier/Corbis Historical/Getty Images; Heritage Images/Hulton Fine Art Collection/Getty Images; John Greim/LightRocket/Getty Images; Barry King/WireImage/Getty Images